# In Search of Sondra

# PALMETTO
### PUBLISHING
Charleston, SC
www.PalmettoPublishing.com

Hardcover ISBN: 979-8-8229-3331-6
Paperback ISBN: 979-8-8229-3332-3

# In Search of

# Sondra

## I, The Journey Within

Poetic Anthology by Sondra Lynn Havard

Edited and Compiled by W. Shaine Nixon

*Sondra Lynn Havard Nixon* was born in Lufkin, Texas, to Hilary Glenn Havard and Mary Marcellette Sanders on January 1, 1949. She graduated from Longview High School, in Longview, Texas, in 1970. At the time, she was twenty years old, pregnant with her first child, and in her second marriage.

On cold, rainy days she loved to curl up by the fire and watch the birds at her feeders. She was a traveling soul and loved the southwest, the Maine woods, and everything Colorado. A beach sunset, sunrise over the mountains, or peaks covered in snow were the things she loved to pursue.

Her persona was brave, strong, and fearless; an independent woman; in reality, she was fragile, gentle and in search of Love, and if she loved you, she loved you unconditionally. She would tell you that her greatest accomplishment in life was the joy she had from raising her two sons and while she loved them above all else, she was completely immersed in her grandchildren and great-grandchildren. As a Maw-Maw, she was at her best. In her, they were spoiled, lived in the greatest stories, had their own personal Halloween Witch, went on magical journeys to the moon and back for infinity and beyond, and if you'd get a line, she'd get a pole. She will forever be missed, forever loved, and forever be in our hearts. Through her stories and travels she will forever be with us in our journeys.

In her own words, "God gave you all to me to cherish. When my time on earth has come and gone, you are never alone. Thank you all for giving me life."

# FOR MY MOTHER

Sondra Lynn Havard Nixon 1949 - 2021
For teaching me
To dream and to love

## DEDICATION

It is important to acknowledge that this journal is dedicated to my children: Marlaina, Mikayla, McKenna, Hunter, and Maleigha. In this journal, I have endeavored to share, convey, and complete what mother could not. She could write it down, but she couldn't communicate it. Thank you for allowing me to be your dad and for sharing in your journey. More importantly, this journal is intended to be something tangible that represents the love and passion that your Maw-Maw Sondra had for all of you. Memories are untouchable, and while I pray they never fade, it's crucial to have something you can feel and hold.

In each of you, I see a piece of her - in your smallest actions, the little sayings, the love you have for those around you, and the intense passion you carry. Always know, she was so proud of all of you.

When you are reading your Maw-Maw's words, it's okay to hear the pain, but also hear the joy and love that she felt for those who touched her heart. She was a complicated and complex person, and each of you shares some part of all those emotions with her. But understand, you brought out the best in her and gave her the unconditional love she desired. You were her entire world, and she loved you unconditionally.

I also want to dedicate this journal to Sondra's sister, Glenna Havard, and her brother, Mark McDaniel. Glenna, you were her first best friend, and you took us in when she needed you most. She loved you. Mark, as her baby brother, she always said you were her first son. You were always there for us. Thank you! While she loved all her siblings, she was closest with you both. She knew you would hold her secrets and help her bury the bodies. In you, she could confide her fears.

Finally, I want to dedicate this journal to my wife, Christi, for being Mother's best friend and putting up with the roller coaster ride of life that mother and I created. She once told me that you were her best friend. She enjoyed your company and shared in your joys and sorrows. She wanted you to have the things she didn't and to always have a place to call home. Life has not always been easy or fair, but together, we have always overcome and persevered. Something she did but did not acknowledge. Thank you for loving us both.

Together, we have all shared some intense moments with mother, and we have come out the better for it with love and respect for each other. Thank you all for giving mother the love she sought and for giving her a reason to feel needed. I'm very proud to call you family, and I truly love each of you.

To The Moon and Back!

# TABLE OF CONTENTS

# I, The Search Within

# INTRODUCTION

Every chapter of my life begins with an ending. I was daddy's little girl. The beautiful, blue eyed blond, who could do no wrong. Everything was as it should be at that time and my life was perfect. The end of that chapter began with "the divorce." My perfect world came crashing down. Reality was thrown in my face like a blast of wind on a January day. My life became dark and cold and wet with tears.

What had I done wrong? Why did this happen? How could I fix it?

The cold wind brushes my cheeks, and a chill runs through my heart, like a hated enemy. Innocence dies somewhere in the mists of revenged hate. I am alone and will spend the better part of the next fifty years learning how to accept that I feel I was born for only one thing; to love and to be loved. In the search for these two things, I have had a long journey.

Two! One step forward and three steps back. One Marriage, One Divorce. One Marriage, One Divorce. One Marriage, One Divorce. It's as if my parent's divorce was the roadmap for the rest of my life. I am following the map! I have left broken hearts and crushed spirits in my wake, but I must keep traveling. Always searching. Always searching. Always longing. Always Alone!

Always just a tear away from happiness. Always wondering what might have been.

## Daddy Broke My Heart

When I was just a little girl
    In my hand I had the world.
But soon my world fell apart.
    My Daddy broke his little girl's heart.
I'm grown now and on my own,
    But I sometimes wish I could go back home.
Of course, that home never did exist.
    It's just a dream and a little girl's wish.

# In The Beginning

## To Live Forever

If I could only put into words,
The emptiness I feel,
When we are apart.
I know you don't feel the same,
But your love is my life.
Please let me live forever!

## The Rivers' Edge

You took my hand and led me down a path,
And laid me on a quilt.
By the river's edge in tall grass,
We made love for hours,
In the hot Texas sun.
That's the day
We became one.
Our minds and our bodies.
Our spirits and our souls.
That's the day
That I became whole!

## Your Strong Hand

I didn't really know you
For the first two years.
But as I got to know you,
My love grew and grew.
When your strong hand
Softly touched mine,
I knew your heart
Was gentle and kind.
One thing that
I surely know,
As time slips by.
Our love
Will grow and grow.
So, please tell this heart of mine
You'll be mine for all time.

## Three Simple Words

Whenever I try to explain
Just how I feel about you.
I find there's really nothing
I can say or do.
There are times I'd like to show,
But I guess you already know
How much that I really care
About the love we share.
Sometimes I wish I could read my mind
And then, I know, that you would find
Due to the way I feel about you
Three simple words will never do.

## Past The River's Edge

There are no echoes now,
As the wind moves,
Through the tall grass.
Only Silence,
And the Pain of the years past!

*Sondra added and changed the verse years after writing the original. She had a habit of reading her poems to herself and self-analyzing where she was in her life. She always questioned "why" things happened and how they could have been different.*

# Wild and Carefree

## Babies, Wild & Carefree

Babies so innocent,
Babies so sweet,
Soft and cuddly,
When sound asleep.

Waite till tomorrow,
Things will change,
They will jumble my mind,
And my house rearrange.

It's really my fault,
This I know,
I should control them,
But I just let them go.

In fact,
I like my babies, wild and carefree.

That's the way I was,
And still try to be.

## Oldsmobile

Time is surely growing near.
To lose her forever,
Is my greatest fear.
Why must she leave me?
What pulls on her heart strings?
Maybe it's just traveling life's unsure road,
And the freedom that it brings.
Does she just love the gypsy life?
Black top
White bottom
Oldsmobile

# Joy

Joy is
     seeing their happy faces.
Joy is
     hearing their laughter.
Joy is
     smelling their sweetness.
Joy is
     the taste of a kiss.
Joy is
     touching their heart.

I am full of Joy.

## I'll Always Love You Son

We'll probably have lots of problems,
      Somewhere down the line.
Your thoughts are too much like your Dads'.
      To get along with mine.
But just remember this one thing.
      After the anger cools,
I'll always, always love you son.
      Even when you act like a fool!

## The Report Card

Today, he brought his report card home,
And, Oh! how proud I was.
Not of the A's and not of the B's,
But of the fact he tried for me.

## Wisteria Hysteria

Mrs. Willoughby had a beautiful yard,
With flowers of every description.
She clipped the hedge, and pruned the rose,
And if one did bleed,
She would have a conniption.
But one warm day, as she tended her yard,
She flew into a maddening whirl.
She said to herself, "I don't need this!"
"What I need is a trip around the world."
She jumped on her bike and flung over her pack.
"I have things to see, and so much to do."
"I have mountains to climb, and seas to part."
"I cannot forever stay here, to watch over you."
Her flowers were taken by shock and surprise.
Some wilted, some fell apart, and some just up and died.
With the exception of one. Her Chinese wisteria.
Which immediately flew into a laughing hysteria.
He crept across the yard and crawled through the fence.
He climbed to the top of the tallest tree.
He followed the roads, lake, and hills, forth hence,
But found nothing of Mrs. Willoughby.

## Lilly White Arms

Tonight, I'd draw neigh,
In her Lilly white arms.

I would lay there all night,
And watch through the window,
Of her soul,
For the dawning of day.

Years of memories come and go.
Simply because I once loved you so.
But this is now,
And that was then.

No longer lovers; merely friends.

# Life – No One Said It Would Be Easy

## Were You Ever Really Mine

You were mine
For such a short time.
Yet etched in my heart,
Forever!

O, the memory!

# I Don't Know Where I'm Going

I don't know where I'm going,
And I don't really care.
Without you there beside me,
      It's likely to be anywhere.
I don't know where I'm going.
I only know where I've been.
I don't want to go back there,
      And be lonely again.
I loved you with all my heart.
I loved you with all my soul.
      And all you did was run around,
And treat me, Oh, so cold.
With all this love, I have to give,
Surely GOD must know,
I cannot go on living.
Without someone to hold.

## Almost Neighbors

We both moved far away.
So, we both could make more pay.
We were almost neighbors.
So strange we never met.

## A Mothers' Prayer

Please let my little boys love life.
Let them hear birds singing every day.
Let them smell the rain before it falls.
Let them see things in the clouds
That make them want to reach the for the stars.
Let them touch the hearts of strangers
As softly as a snowflake falls.
Let them taste the bitterness of life
So the sweetness will be even sweeter.
Please let my little boys love life
And answer a Mother's Prayer.

## When You're Feeling Low

I know that you have been feeling low,
And things are going very slow.
But one day soon
The sun will shine,
And just because
          You
Are a friend of mine,
I'll say a prayer,
To **GOD** above.
To shine down on you
With all his love.
So, when you are feeling a little low,
And things are going very slow,
Remember what friends are for.

For my boys – with Mothers' Love

# For my brother!

Slade, not a day goes by that I don't think about the times we shared. When I look at all the pictures of us growing up, you made her smile. She never ended a conversation without asking had I spoken with you and that I needed to call you. You see, you were always in her thoughts. In you, she saw daddy. She told me this. Her exact words were, "you were quiet in your feelings."

We both know who got the gift for gab.

She didn't always have the answers, but she always had time, especially for you. Time to listen, time to visit, and love beyond measure. She loved to share your successes. I miss her too.

I love you brother! You made her proud!

## Shaine & Slade

You are the sunshine
    In my life.
You are the laughter
    In my heart.
You are my dreams
    Come true.


I love you. Wherever you are, I am with you.
    Mother

## Looking To Tomorrow

He says they need disappointments.
So they can learn to grow.
I say this is something
They really don't need to know.
If we teach them to love, and
How not to hate,
I think we will have taught them
The way through
The Golden Gate.
Life doesn't have to be
Dread and sorrow.
It can be things like happiness,
And looking forward
To tomorrow.

## Sleeping Boys

As I sit here and watch my sleeping boys,
I wonder what fate in life they will meet.
Will they be loud, noisy, and rude,
Or will they be wild, handsome, and crude?
Will they be good, healthy, and true,
Or will they be bad, sickly, and blue?
Will they have song, and laughter, and life,
Or will they have misery, suffering, and strife?
Only GOD knows the answer to these,
But anything is better than being like me.

## How I Love My Boys

They're my sunshine,
      And my rain.
They're my laughter,
      And my pain.
They're my joy,
      And my sorrow.
They're my yesterday,
      And my tomorrow.
They're my beginning,
      And my end.
And I'm their mother,
      And forever friend.

## Three Boys

How much I do love
My three beautiful boys.
The laughter in their blue eyes.
The teasing in their tender voices.
The gentleness in their touch.
The warmth in their hearts.
How much I do love
My two Sons
And their Daddy.

# Thoughts in the Night

# Thoughts

Thoughts come to me in the middle of the night.
Thoughts of years long since passed.
Thoughts of dreams I thought would last.
Thoughts of dreams that did not pass.
When the house is still and quiet,
Thoughts of laughter and thoughts of tears.
Thoughts that were hidden all these years.
But they come to me in the middle of the night,
When the house is still and my mind quiet

## Don't Despair

Don't despair!
Tomorrows light will light the night,
And the darkness will turn to day,
And our fears will all go away.

## What You Do to Me

What you do to me
Without realizing it
Really amazes me.
For never before have I felt this way.

When I see you smile,
I can't help but smile.
And when I hear your laughter,
Somehow, I can't help but laugh.

The simple expressions you make,
While hard at work.
Seem to make me so happy,
And love you even more.

Often while you're telling me something,
I just sit and watch your eyes grow big.
Your voice grows louder.
Then I wonder how I ever did without you.

As I think about you,
I wonder if you know
The things you do to me.
That only you can do.

## The Shape of Day

The day is new,
And across the grass
There's a fresh smell of dew.
The day is young,
And across the forest
Things begin to move.
Like the small bird
Fluttering in the trees,
Or a gray squirrel
On a tree trunk,
And the rustling of leaves.
And above, all that's below,
The day takes shape.

It's August 1985

# Freedom

The look in your eyes.
The touch of your hand.
The warmth of your kiss.
I ask no more than this.

But greater than my need for you,
Is my love for you,
And my wish for your happiness.
And if my love is not right for you,
I can give you your happiness.

By giving you, your freedom!

# The End of Love

## Memories

Years of memories
Come and go,
Because I loved
You so.
But this is now,
And that was then.
So, why don't
We just be friends.

## Hurt Again

I was hurt.
The years were long and lonely.
There seemed no way I could go on.
Then you came into my life.
I learned to laugh and love again.
I learned to live again.
And by losing you,
I learned to hurt again.

## Waiting on Fall

In winter
    I am happy.
In spring
    I do delight.
In summer
    I grow tired.
In fall
    He will call.

## Without You

I set alone in my room at night.
Waiting for day.
Hoping things will be right.
But without your love,
All is lost.
Morning brings another day.
I set alone in my room at night.

## Set Them Free

If you love someone, set them free.
If they come back, they belong to you.
If the never come back,
They never really belonged to you at all.

## Unbearable Pain

My empty heart aches,
From your memory.
The tears sting my eyes,
And gently run down my cheeks.
Your smile flashes through my heart.
The pain is unbearable.

## To See Life and To Love

My green-eyed gypsy woman,
Green eyes full of fire.
Green eyes full of fire.
Long locks flowing free.
Long locks flowing free.
Want ... stay here with me.
I've offered her my mansion.
My gold and all my love.
But she says she's driven,
By spirits from up above.
She must keep on moving.
To see life and to love.
Oh! To see life and to love.
Why can't you settle down?
Oh! Why can't you settle down?
Don't ... roam from town to town.
The parting of her hour.

## Love Must End

I don't know where we're going,
And I don't know where we've been.

I only know we were strangers, and now,
We're more than friends.

Life has many directions,
And, also, its ups and downs.

But with you by my side,
I can take life in full stride.

I don't know where I am going.
I don't know where I've been.

I only know, I loved you once,
And now that love must end.

## Goodbye My Love

My Heart lies in the shadows,
Just waiting for your touch.

My heart lies in the shadows,
It's loving you so much.

My heart lies in the shadows.
Without your love I'll die.

My Heart lies in the shadows.
Goodbye my love, goodbye.

## Embers

The days of our love were few,
But our love was so special.
I'll always remember you.
The walks in the park.
The talks after dark.
That flirtatious wink that made me think
I'm the luckiest girl in the world.
The tears we've shared and especially the laughter.
I'll remember these things for ever after.
Even after the warm glow of our love
Has burned to embers.
Even after the four winds of our love
Blow the cool ashes of my life away.

# To The Moon and Back

*For My Grandkids*

## Your Mother

The angels touched your mother.
On the day she was born,
The sun was surely shining
On such a glorious morn.

Her sweet and gentle nature.
Her kind and loving way.
With her to guide you,
You will possess these things.
Someday!

There may be times you disagree,
And think that she's not fair.
But she will always love you,
And give you the very best care.

So, when your life feels stormy,
And I know it surely will,
Just remember the angel's decision
To put you in your Mother's care.

For My M & M's
Love Maw-Maw

# Granddaughters

They are angels sent from above.
To touch my heart and teach me to love.
Until you've held them in your arms,
You can't imagine all their charms.
There are no words to describe your emotion.
Well, maybe two.
Complete Devotion.

Granddaughters!

For my M & M's
I Love you to the moon and back.

Maw-Maw

## A Daughter Like You

Love your **MOM** with all your heart,
And let her be your friend,
Because she'll always love you so,
And stand by you through thick and thin.

She may not let you do the things
You really want to do.
But it's for the best,
And someday you'll agree too.

When you have a daughter like you.

## To Marlaina

I hold your hand,
And kiss your face.
For in my heart,
You have a special place.
A place where laughter
Sings loud and clear.
A place where you are,
Oh, so dear.
And though we are miles apart,
You always have a special place.
In my heart!

I Love you always,
Maw-Maw

## To Mikayla

When you look at me,
With those big blue eyes,
I wonder,
If you see into my soul.
You are such a wise little girl
To only be three years old.

Love you always. To the moon and back.

Maw-Maw

# On Pride and Death

## ONLY PRIDE

The gentle rain on the window pain
Only brings my tears, for many lost years,
We could have shared.
If only pride had been set aside,
You would be here with me,
And our boys.

The miles are many now, between us.
But you are never out of my heart.
I'll love you all my eternity.

Why did our dream go by so fast?
Was it too beautiful to last?

So many things left undone,
Except loving you, and our two sons,
And if nothing else can be said about me,
Let it be said that I loved you Three.

# Enduring

The winds of time blow softly,
And memories of the past,
Drift into my thoughts.
My heart aches,
For what might have been,
But will never be.
Our life together,
Was the blink of an eye,
The beat of a heart,
The drop of a tear.
Oh! So brief!
But, Oh, so powerful.
There will never be
Another moment in time,
As enduring.
I miss you,
With every breath I take,
And pray this one will be my last.


January 2007

## The Sunshine That We Shared

As I lay dying in my bed,
Don't be sorrowful.
Hold up your head.
Dry your tears,
And remember,
All the laughing years.
And all the sunshine we have shared.

I Love You,
Sondra

"God gave you all to me to cherish. When my time on earth has come and gone, you are never alone. Thank you all for giving me life."

To those of you who took the time to not only hear, but listen to Sondra's voice, thank you. My hope is that you gain insight into the trauma that she felt but leave knowing her passion for love and family. At some point in all our lives, we have felt some form of connection with her. We all share in this human experience and "**we all experience trauma**" in our own way, but she told us we can overcome trauma through unconditional love.

Generational trauma, exists! How we deal with situations, loss, love, emotion, passion and especially anger can be triggered at any age. For Sondra "The Divorce" came early and set the precedent for the rest of her life. I know. I lived it.

When my parents divorced, I was eight years old. Funny, or ironic, I don't remember moving. I only remember waking up and not being! Everything changed! I was no longer *her* little boy. I had to step up. Be the man of the house. Protect her and my brother. Those first three years were unimaginable. But she was determined to provide for us.

I could not share or write this for her when she was still with me. The words would not come. I'm sorry for that mother, but I know you understood it in your heart. Unwritten, and Unsaid things that don't need spoken. Memories that burn in your mind with every breath. We share so many of the same emotions, passions, desires, and longing for "what if" "what could have been?" Always Searching!

Thank you for the journey, both good and bad. For without those experiences, I would not be the man I am today. Rest easy mother. I got this.

Your Loving Son,

# I've Watched You Sleeping Oft

I've watched you sleeping oft
And listened to your tears
I've held your hand throughout the night
And listened to your fears
I've combed your hair and held your hand
And told you it would all be right
And in the darkness of your soul
We made it through the night
There were many times
When things did not go right
That fear took over your heart
But you, In Full Mother Mode
Never gave up the fight
Regardless of what we had
Or how little it really was
It never really mattered
Cause our house was filled with love
Not the kind of love that's shallow
And others see as fake
But the Purist of love
A Mother's Love
That's deep, and Never Goes Away!

# ABOUT THE AUTHOR

 W. Shaine Nixon, a native of Longview, Texas, embodies a life rich in diverse experiences, education, and a profound connection to the great outdoors. Born on January 21, 1969, Nixon's journey encompasses a spectrum of roles, from dedicated educator to outdoor enthusiast.

Graduating from East Texas Baptist University in 1996 and subsequently earning a Master's in Education from Stephen F. Austin State University, Nixon dedicated 16 years to shaping young minds in Texas public schools. His roles included teaching high school English, coaching various sports, and even assuming the responsibilities of a school principal.

Nixon's professional journey took an adventurous turn when he moved to Alaska in 2018, assuming the role of Principal at the Andrew K. Demoski School in the Yukon Koyukuk School District. In 2022, he transitioned to the Southeast Island School District on Prince of Wales Island, covering seven campuses on one of America's largest islands. His leadership in education reflects not only his commitment to academic excellence but also his ability to adapt to diverse and challenging environments.

Beyond the confines of education, Nixon is a family man and an avid outdoorsman. Married to Christi Nixon for over 34 years, he is the proud father of five and grandfather to eight. Nixon's love for the outdoors is deeply rooted, evident in his years as a licensed Big Game Guide in New Mexico and the owner-operator of World Slam Outfitters from 1999 to 2008.

An accomplished individual, Nixon's passion for hunting, guiding, and the spiritual connection he finds in nature have significantly shaped his worldview. *In Search of Sondra: I, The Journey Within* marks his debut in the literary world, a poignant biography that reflects not only his storytelling prowess but also his profound understanding of the human experience. Nixon's journey is one of service, leadership, and a deep connection with the natural world—a journey that continues to unfold with every chapter of his life.

Milton Keynes UK
Ingram Content Group UK Ltd.
UKHW050653250124
436483UK00017B/208/J

9 798822 933316